Do Monsters Exist?

Sarah Fleming

OXFORD
University Press

OXFORD
UNIVERSITY PRESS

Great Clarendon Street, Oxford OX2 6DP

Oxford University Press is a department of the University of Oxford.
It furthers the University's objective of excellence in research, scholarship,
and education by publishing worldwide in

Oxford   New York

Auckland   Cape Town   Dar es Salaam   Hong Kong   Karachi
Kuala Lumpur   Madrid   Melbourne   Mexico City   Nairobi
New Delhi   Shanghai   Taipei   Toronto

With offices in

Argentina   Austria   Brazil   Chile   Czech Republic   France   Greece
Guatemala   Hungary   Italy   Japan   Poland   Portugal   Singapore
South Korea   Switzerland   Thailand   Turkey   Ukraine   Vietnam

Oxford is a registered trade mark of Oxford University Press
in the UK and in certain other countries

British Library Cataloguing in Publication Data

Data available

ISBN 978-0-19-919862-7

9 10

Printed in China by Imago

Paper used in the production of this book is a natural,
recyclable product made from wood grown in sustainable forests.
The manufacturing process conforms to the environmental
regulations of the country of origin

Acknowledgements

The publisher would like to thank the following for permission to reproduce
photographs: p5 Bettmann/Corbis (top), Tim Davis/Corbis; p6 BBC Photo Library; p7 Sandra
Mansi/Getty Images (top), Martin Rogers/Corbis; p9 Dave Rubert Photography; p16 Jason
Hawkes/Corbis (top), Science Photo Library; p18 Vo Trung Dung/Corbis Sygma; p19
Reuters/Corbis; p20 Patricia & Angus MacDonald/Aerographica; p21 Bryan & Cherry
Alexander/John Hyde; p22 Vo Trung Dung/Corbis Sygma, p23 Ralph White/Corbis

Cover photo: Fortean Picture Library

Illustrations by Stefan Chabluk and Kevin Jenkins

Design by Andy Wilson

Contents

Introduction

Have you heard of the Yeti? Bigfoot? The Loch Ness monster? Do you think they are real – that they **exist**? They are all examples of monsters which *some* people say are real, but there is not enough **proof** for everyone to agree.

Monsters like these are called cryptids*. In this book we'll take a look at some of these animals, and the reports about them. With enough proof, some of these cryptids may be named as 'real' animals, in the future.

There are cryptids all over the world. They may be huge or hairy, they may eat humans or sing, but they all have some things in common:

- they're difficult to find

- there is no scientific proof that they exist.

*__Cryptid:__ an animal that some people say is alive and real, but there is not enough proof about it for **scientists** to agree.

* from the Greek Kruptos = hidden or secret

What kind of proof do scientists need?

Reports of **sightings**, blurred photos, or **casts** of footprints are not good enough proof for a scientist. This kind of proof can be faked, or there can be different explanations, for example, the glimpse of a 'Bigfoot' could be the glimpse of a bear.

A body (live or dead) is the best proof of the existence of a creature; then tests can be carried out to see if it really is a new kind of animal.

Casts of large footprints

The okapi was thought to be a cryptid until 1901. Local people had hunted okapi for hundreds of years, but it was only when someone took an okapi body to show scientists that it was finally **officially** recognized as being a real animal.

Hoax in the works

It is difficult to prove whether cryptids are real or not because they are difficult to find. Proving their existence is made even *more* difficult because of hoaxes.

A hoax makes people believe something that is not true. People make up hoaxes about lots of things. They can be good jokes, or they can cause other people harm.

April Fool's Day, 1957.
In a famous hoax, a TV show said that spaghetti grew on trees!

Why do people make up hoaxes about cryptids?

Some do it

- for fun
- for money
- to be on TV
- to show off
- because they like to make fun of other people
- because they want to give other people some 'proof' to make them believe in something.

This is a picture of 'something' in a lake. For thirty years, people have argued about what it shows. Is it a monster? Is it **driftwood**? Is it a hoax? Since the photo was taken, more than 130 people have reported seeing a monster in this lake. No one reported seeing one *before* it was taken.

What do *you* think?

Lake Champlain, USA, 1977

Driftwood

Sorting out the truth from the made-up makes it even more difficult for scientists to decide if a cryptid is real or not.

I'm an ape man

All over the world people report seeing cryptid apes. Apes walk on two feet and also use their knuckles. Officially, humans are the only relative of the ape that walks upright … but are there others?

A dwarf ape: Orang-pendek

Only 1 metre tall, this cryptid has long head-hair which can be anything from black to blond. It is very strong – 'built like a boxer', one eyewitness said.

There have been many sightings, by locals and scientists. Hairs have been found in trees at a height of about 1 metre. 15 centimetre-long footprints have been found that are not a human child's. The jungle is remote, which means the Orang-pendek is less likely to be disturbed, and the local people believe it is a real animal.

Country	Habitat	Evidence	Known hoaxes	Chance of being real
Sumatra	Jungle	Hair, footprints, sighting by scientist	None known	High

Orang-utan means 'man of the forest' and 'Orang-pendek' means 'small man'. Can you work out which bit of the word means 'man'?

Bigfoot = big ape!

Country	Habitat	Evidence	Known hoaxes	Chance of being real
China	Remote mountains	Footprints	Many known	Low

Bigfoot is one of the most famous 'ape men' in the world. People from many native tribes in North America believe that a Bigfoot has existed for over 1000 years. But there are so many Bigfoot hoaxes that it's hard to find the truth.

Sandal hoax

This man made 'Bigfoot' tracks. But he could not have made all the thousands of tracks found all over North America.

Hoax of a hoax?

Roger Patterson claimed to have filmed a Bigfoot in 1977. Then, in 2004, Robert Heironimus said that *he* was the Bigfoot in the film – in an ape suit! Some people, though, say that Robert is the hoaxer, and the film is of a real Bigfoot!

Case study 1: Mokele-mbembe

Cameroon
Congo
Gabon

The story

You're deep in the jungle, fishing on a boat. Suddenly a creature erupts from the water. The boat tips up. One man is bitten in two; another is beaten to death by the monster's huge tail. As abruptly as it arrived, the monster silently submerges…

Sauropod dinosaurs lived 200 to 70 million years ago. But could they still exist in the vast swamps of the congo?

The reports

Mokele-mbembe (say 'mock–ay–lay–um–bem–bay') is said to look like a dinosaur. Between 5–10 metres in length, it has a long tail, long neck and small head. It is a plant-eater, but will kill animals that get too close. It has been sighted killing hippopotamuses, and overturning boats. It has bitten or hit people to death with its tail, but it does not eat the bodies.

Chance of being real
Low

The place

In the Congo there is a swamp that is over 140,000 square kilometres – twice the size of Ireland (Eire). Mokele-mbembe is said to live there, using rivers through the swamp as roads. Mokele-mbembe means 'one that stops the flow of rivers.'

FACT OR FICTION?

The swamp is so big that 80% of it has never been explored, so strange new creatures might live there. Local people have drawn pictures of Mokele–mbembe that look like a sauropod dinosaur. Huge footprints, 30–90 centimetres in diameter with three claws, have been found. The distance between the prints is over 2 metres!

The story

You wake one morning and go to tend your animals. But there lies your goat, with two or three perfect round holes in its neck. There's no blood – it's been sucked dry!

Chance of being real

Low/medium

The reports

Locals call the creature Chupacabras which means 'goat sucker'. Its slanting eyes look like an **alien's**, its body is a bit like a dinosaur's. It mostly walks on two legs, but has been seen on four. It can leap over trees – some even say it can fly! It kills without frightening its prey, sinking either its fangs (two holes) or its claws (three holes in a triangle) into the neck.

The place

The goat sucker is reported to have been seen in many country farming areas in middle America.

FACT OR FICTION?

Over 2,000 sightings of the goat sucker have been reported in the last ten years alone. It is said to have killed thousands of goats, chickens and other livestock over the last 50 years. Some say the animals are killed by wild dogs, or baboons. Some believe that the animal is a cross between an alien and an animal which was made secretly by American scientists but has escaped...

Case study 3: Death worm

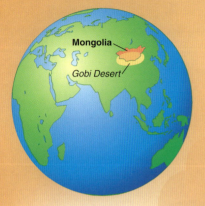

Mongolia
Gobi Desert

The story

It lurks under the sand, moving beneath your feet. Suddenly its head erupts from the surface, spitting deadly poison!

The reports

A stocky, blood-red worm, usually about 1.5 metres long, with spikes at both ends. Some say it kills by squirting poison at its prey, others that it gives a deadly electric shock. It kills from a distance of several metres.

The place

The Death Worm is said to live in the Gobi desert and sleeps underground for most of the year. It has been sighted only in June and July – the hottest months – when it is said to come to the surface after it has been raining.

Chance of being real
Medium

FACT OR FICTION?

The desert is huge and few people live there, so there may be a new type of animal that is yet to be discovered. The Death Worm could be some kind of snake, or legless lizard.

The Death Worm has only ever been seen by local people, but there are many recorded sightings, and the details are very similar in each case. And something must account for the strange deaths of animals and even some people in the area...

The Loch Ness Monster:
an in-depth study

There are legends about monsters that live in lakes all over the world. The most famous monster is in Scotland.

Sea reptile. Up to 11 metres long. Lived in the time of the dinosaurs. 200–65 million years ago.

The cryptid

Most people think that the Loch Ness monster ('Nessie') is a long-necked, small headed sea reptile called a plesiosaur (say 'plee–zee–oh–SAW').

The habitat

Loch Ness has more water in it than all the other lakes in Britain put together. There is so much water you could hide all the people in the world in it *three times over*. So even if there were *thirty* monsters in the lake, it would be hard to find them.

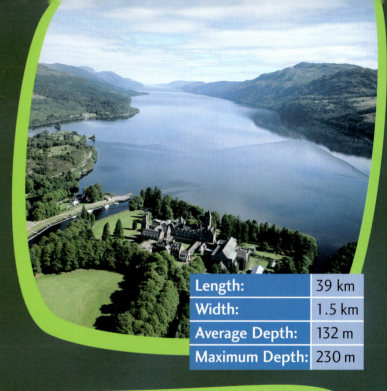

Length:	39 km
Width:	1.5 km
Average Depth:	132 m
Maximum Depth:	230 m

Sightings

One of the first sightings was by St Columba in AD 565. Legend says he saved someone from a monster that lived in the river that flows from Loch Ness to the sea. Over 10 000 people say they have seen the Loch Ness Monster. Some even say it has crossed the road in front of their cars!

'Nessie' Hoaxes

The truth about whether there is a cryptid in Loch Ness has been muddled up by lots of hoaxes. Here are some.

The first 'Nessie' Hoax

In 1933 a new road made it easier to get to the loch, and this photo was taken. But in 1994 the people who made this 'Nessie' admitted it was a hoax – just a piece of plastic attached to a toy submarine!

They put the monster in the lake. It made the children laugh.
"It looks brilliant!" said Chip.

"What a good joke," said Biff. "What a good joke to play on Mum."

14

15

There are even hoaxes in fiction books!

Fossil hoax

Do you think this newspaper cutting confirms that 'Nessie' is a dinosaur?

16 July 2003

Nessie's bones found?

Do the fossilised neck bones of a Jurassic sea reptile, found in Loch Ness by a tourist, belong to the original Loch Ness monster?

Experts from the National Museum of Scotland say that the fossil is real. But they are puzzled that it was found in Loch Ness. Plesiosaurus fossils have been found on the coast 50km away, but

never before in Loch Ness.

'I tripped over the fossil in the water,' said pensioner Gerald McSorley, who found the...

The fossil is real, but scientists have discovered that it doesn't come from Loch Ness – the type of stone that the fossil bones are set in is not found in Loch Ness. The fossil was probably put there by a hoaxer. It was found in one of the few places where tourists can get down to the loch side.

Is 'Nessie' a Dinosaur?

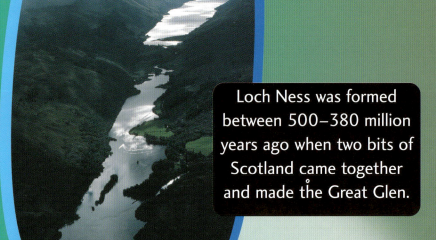

Loch Ness was formed between 500–380 million years ago when two bits of Scotland came together and made the Great Glen.

ARGUMENTS
FOR

Everyone agrees that 'Nessie' has a plesiosaur shape. But how could there be a plesiosaur in Loch Ness?

1 Some people say that a plesiosaur ('Nessie') was trapped in Loch Ness when it was formed and is still alive today.

2 Some say that a *group* of plesiosaurs was trapped, and the family has continued ever since. If this is right, then 'Nessie' (or a group of 'Nessies') wouldn't have to be millions of years old.

A glacier bigger than this helped to carve out the Loch.

ARGUMENTS AGAINST

1 Plesiosaurs didn't exist until 200 million years ago – *after* the Great Glen was formed.

2 65 million years ago something happened on Earth which killed off all the dinosaurs and sea reptiles.

3 12 000 years ago Loch Ness was under *1.2 kilometres of ice!*

4 Plesiosaurs lived in salt water – Loch Ness is fresh water.

5 If one plesiosaur was trapped, it would be millions of years old!

6 Loch Ness is very cold and dark. There is not enough food in the lake to feed a group of plesiosaurs.

7 Plesiosaurs breathed air, so they would have to come to the surface often. 'Nessie' isn't seen often enough to be an air-breathing creature.

'Nessie' could be...

'Nessie' could be...	But...
a family of otters	would they be big enough?
driftwood	it doesn't swim against the current.
one or more long-necked seals	would they be big enough?
strange wave patterns	where is 'Nessie's' head?
a large sturgeon fish	no skeletons have ever been found.
a prehistoric whale trapped in the lake	whales are salt water animals.
an extra large eel	would it be big enough?

Is 'Nessie' an eel?

Chances of 'Nessie' being a dinosaur	Chances of 'Nessie' being a monster	Chances of 'Nessie' being *something* real!
Low	Low	Medium

Normal European eels only grow to be 1 metre long. But sometimes eels can grow very big. Eels have gills and breathe underwater, so they don't come to the surface very often. This **behaviour** would fit with the few sightings of 'Nessie'. Eels sometimes cross land, so they could have been seen crossing a road. *But* could an eel grow big enough to be mistaken for a monster?

Underwater cameras have found eels in Loch Ness. Have one or two grown into monsters?

Remember – new animals are discovered every year. 'Nessie' could still exist! What do *you* think?

Glossary

alien – foreign or unnatural – not of this world

behaviour – the way someone or something acts

cast – shape made by pouring liquid metal or plaster into a mould

driftwood – wood floating on a sea or lake, or washed ashore

evidence – anything that gives people reason to believe something

exist – be present as part of what is real

fossil – the remains or traces of a prehistoric animal or plant. Once buried in the ground for a very long time, it becomes hardened in rock.

habitat – where an animal or plant lives naturally

officially – done or said by someone with authority

proof – a fact or event that shows that something is true

scientist – someone who studies the physical world by means of observation and experiment

sighting – when something is seen

Index